Movie Duets

ARRANGED BY CAROL KLOSE

This publication is not for sale in
the E.C. and/or Australia
or New Zealand.

ISBN 0-7935-3993-5

HAL•LEONARD™
CORPORATION
7777 W. BLUEMOUND RD. P.O. BOX 13819 MILWAUKEE, WI 53213

CHARIOTS OF FIRE
from CHARIOTS OF FIRE

Music by VANGELIS

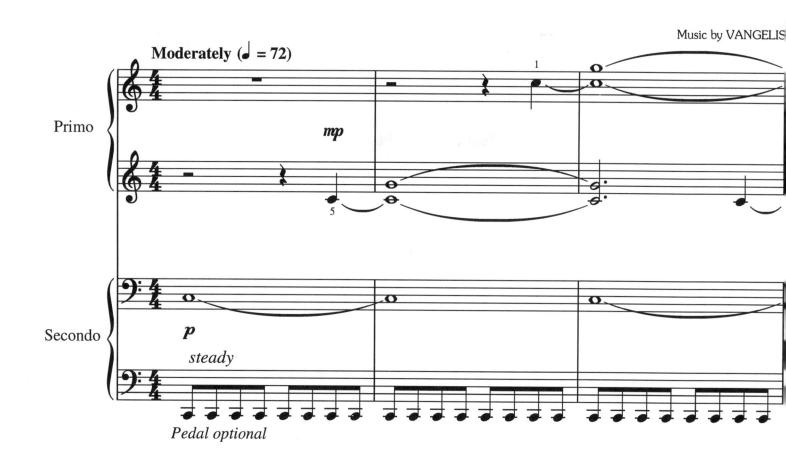

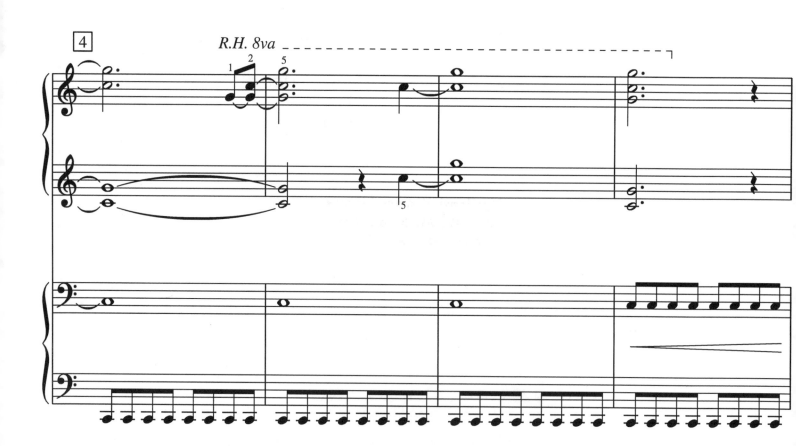

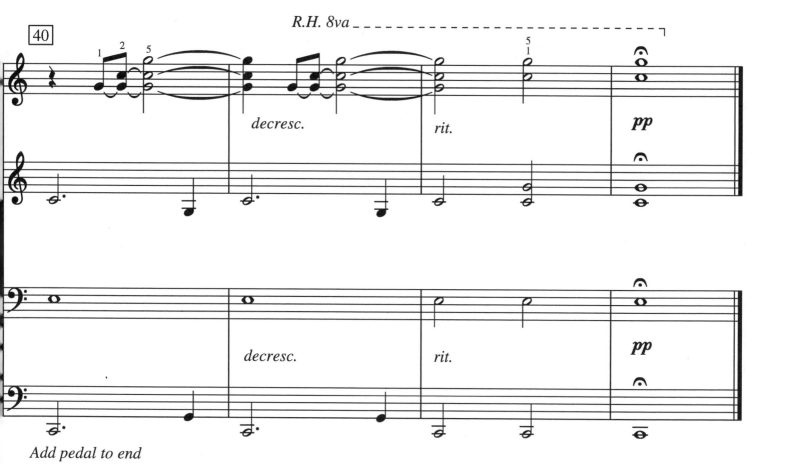

Add pedal to end

LOVE THEME
from CINEMA PARADISO

Music by ANDREA MORRICONE

With expression ($\textbf{\textit{d}}$ = 100-104)

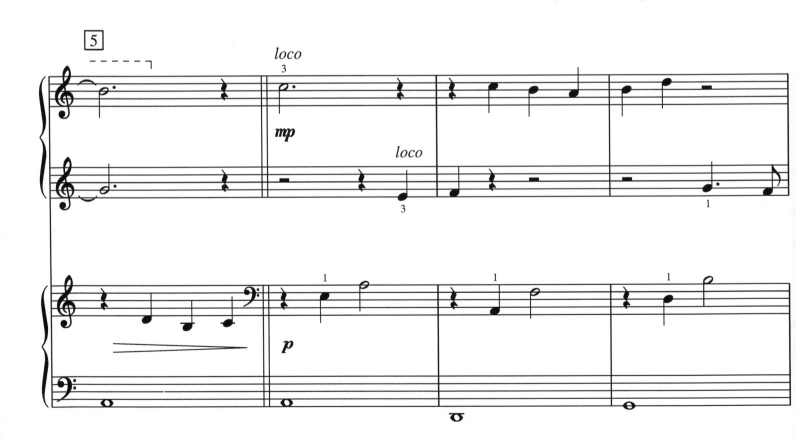

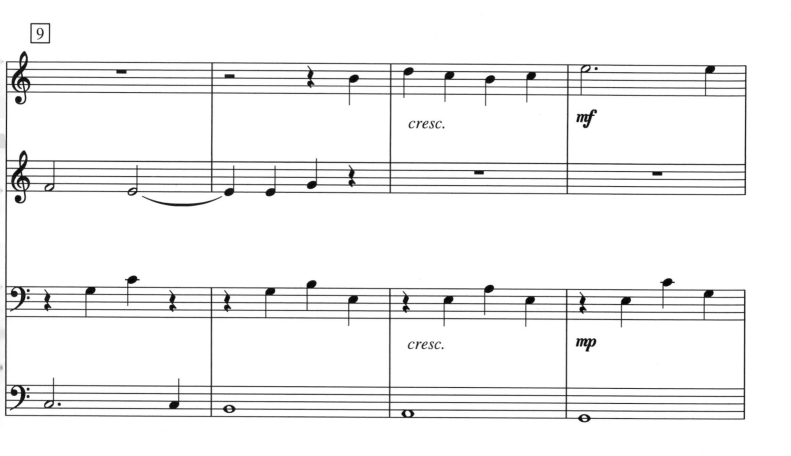

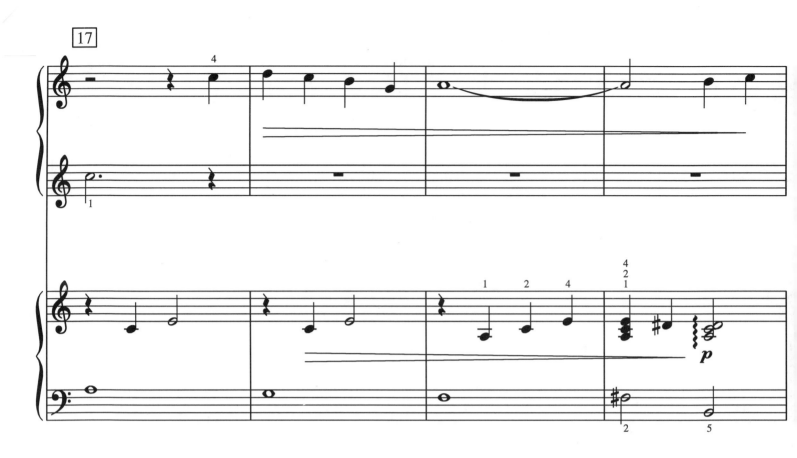

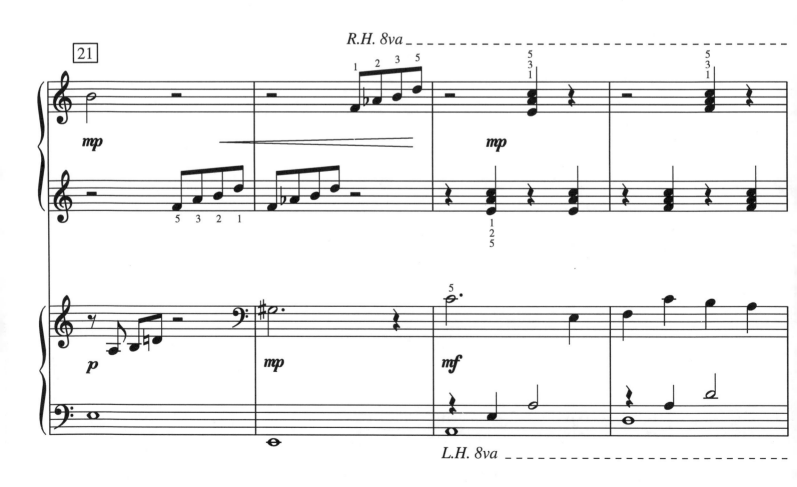

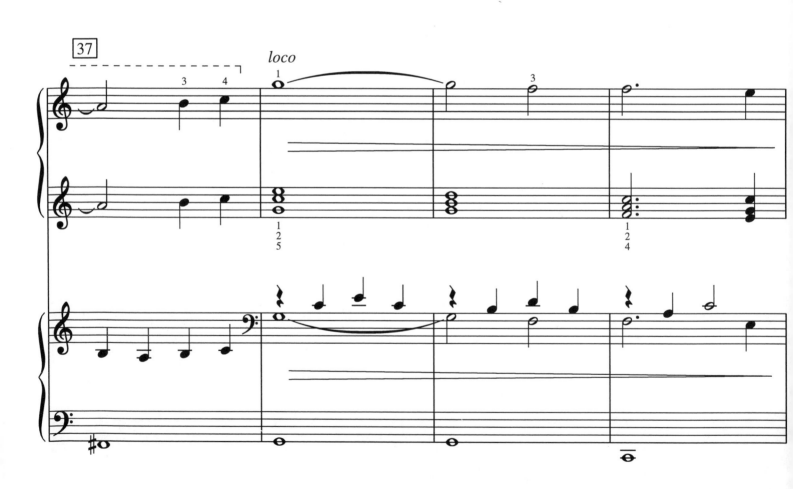

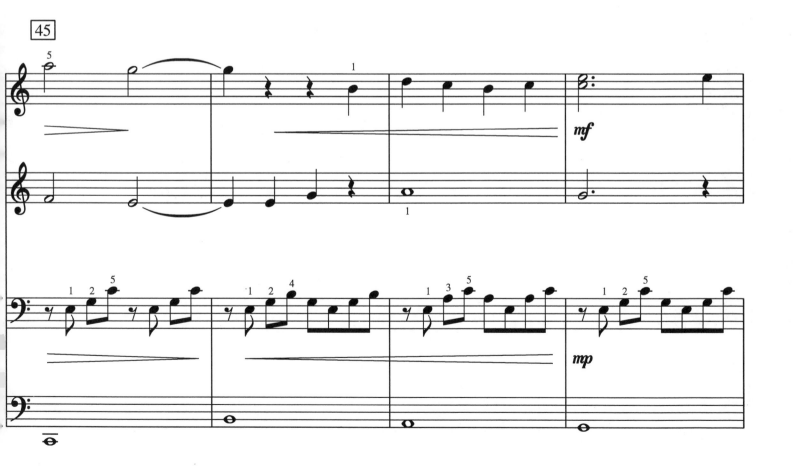

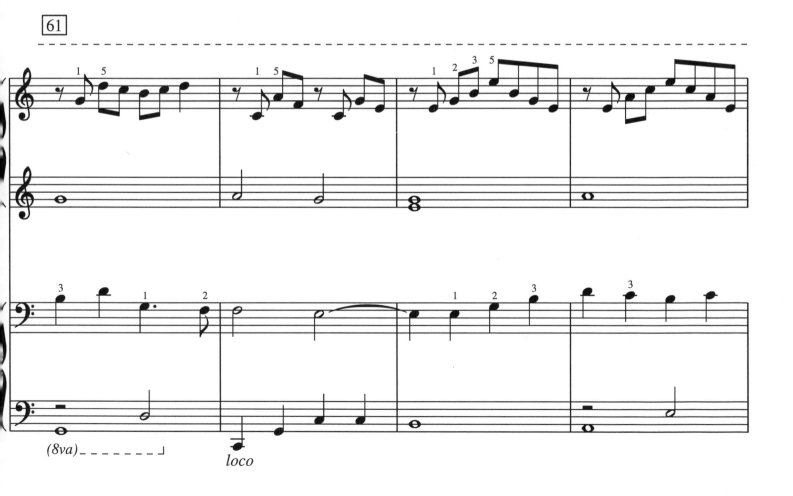

THEME FROM
E.T. (THE EXTRA-TERRESTRIAL)

from the Universal Picture E.T. (THE EXTRA-TERRESTRIAL)

Music by JOHN WILLIAMS

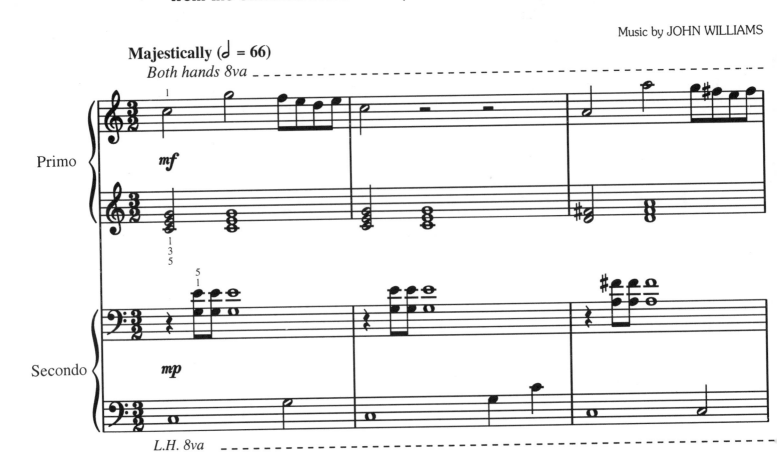

MCA music publishing

19

(Both hands 8va)

(L.H. 8va)

22

R.H. 8va

loco

Both hands 8va

(L.H. 8va)

29

loco

(L.H. 8va) _

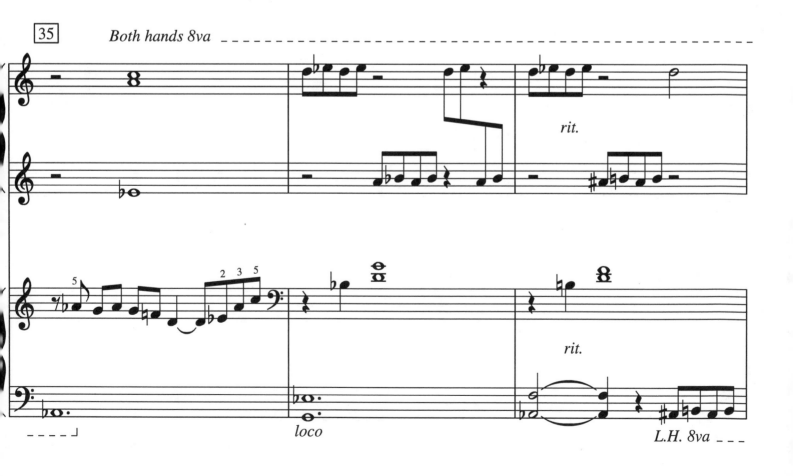

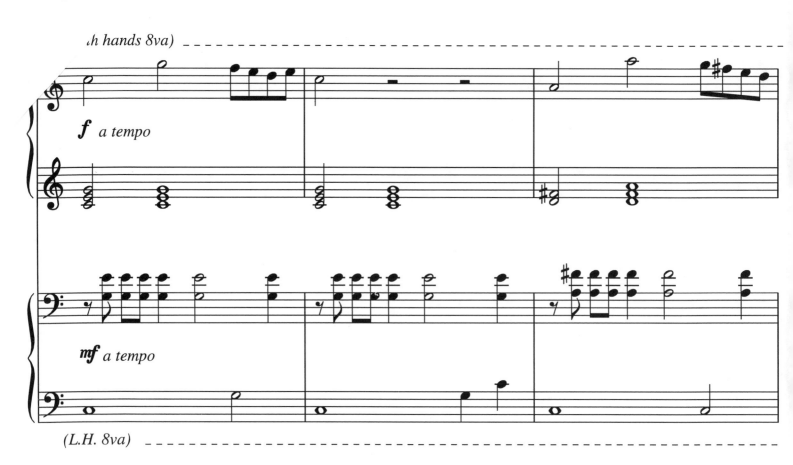

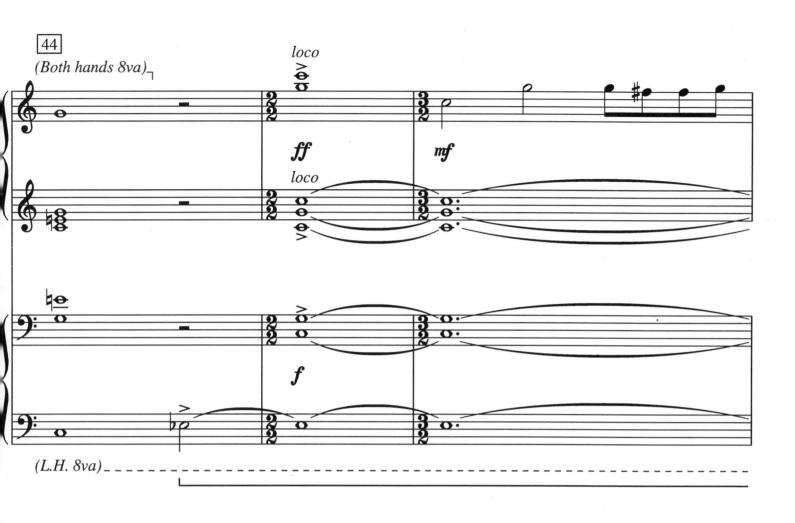

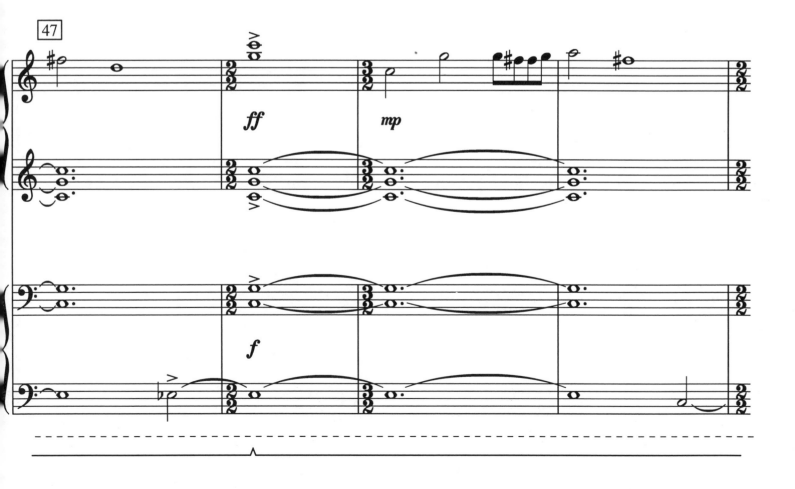

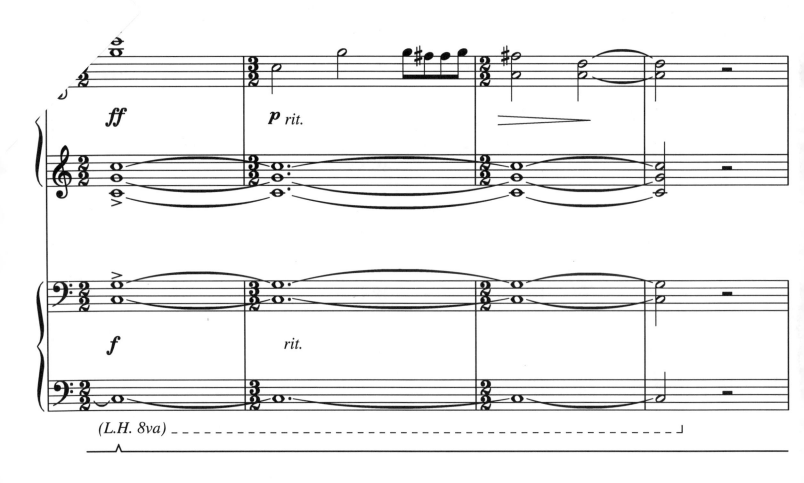

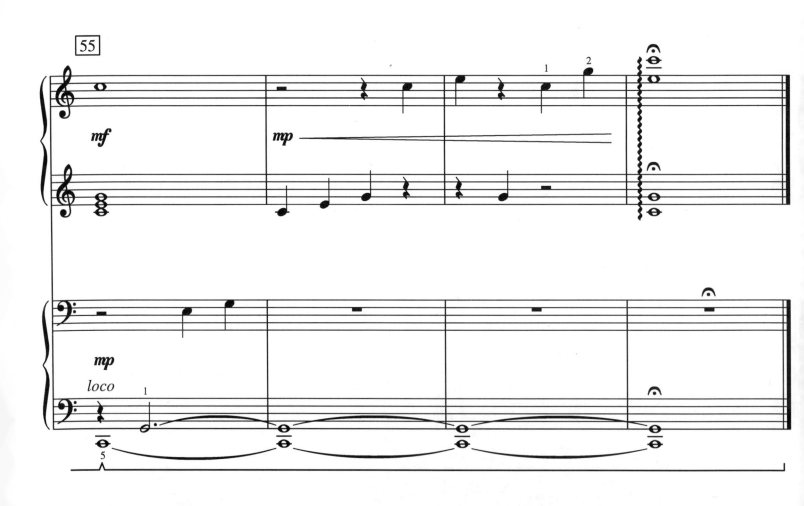

THE EXODUS SONG

from EXODUS

Words by PAT BOONE
Music by ERNEST GOLD

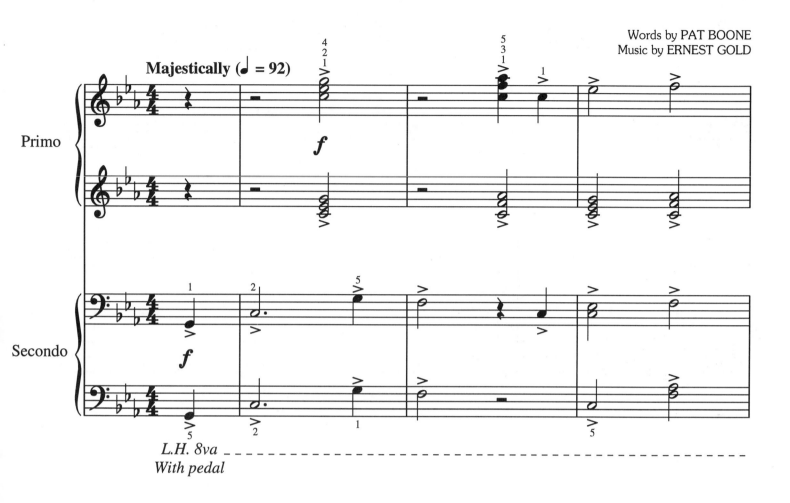

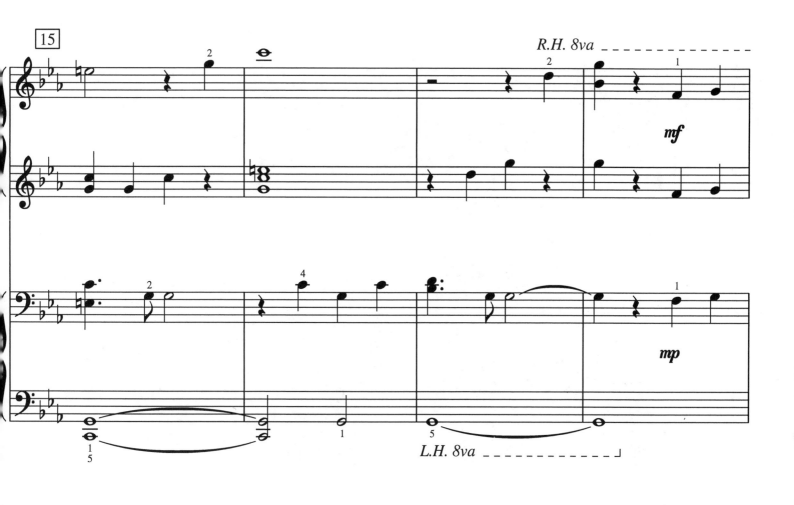

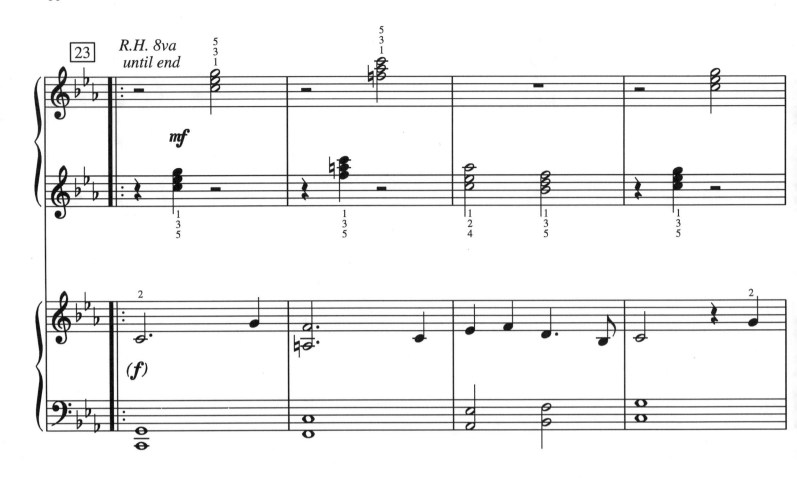

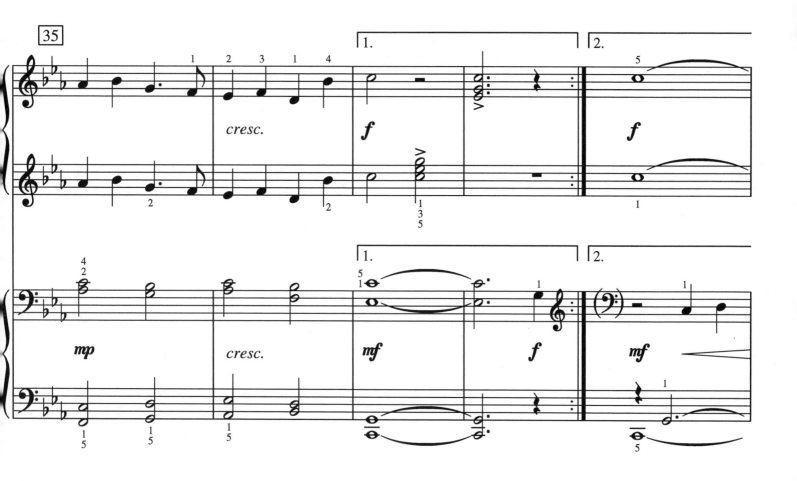

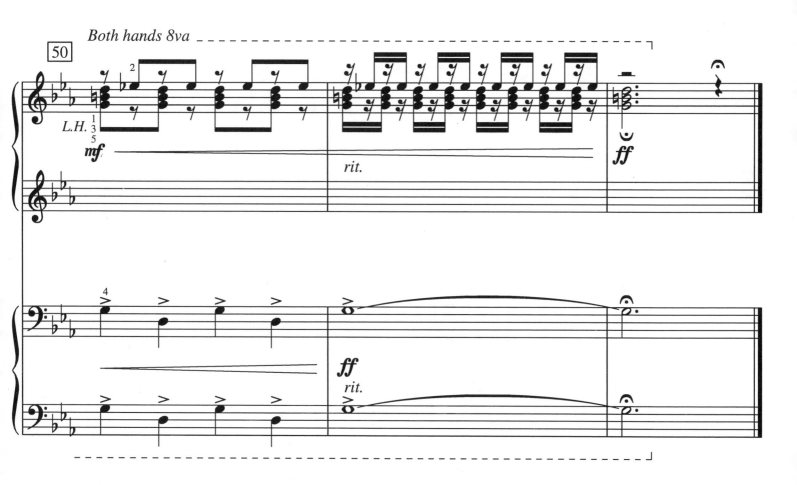

THE GODFATHER
(Love Theme)
from the Paramount Picture THE GODFATHER

By NINO ROTA

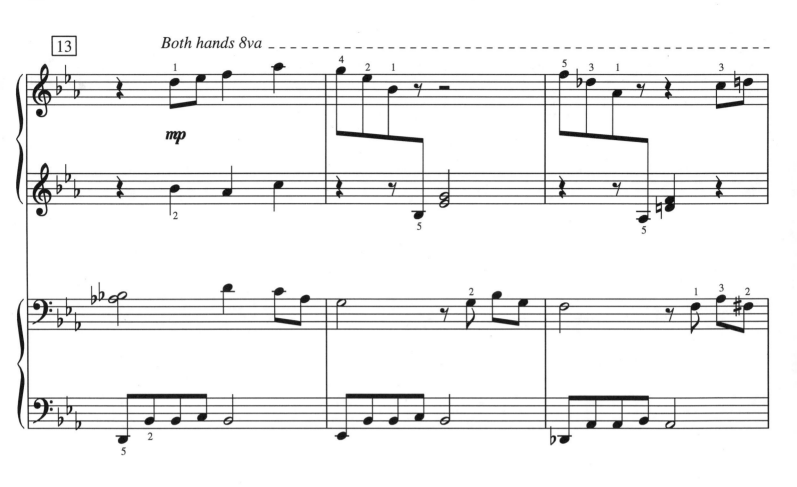

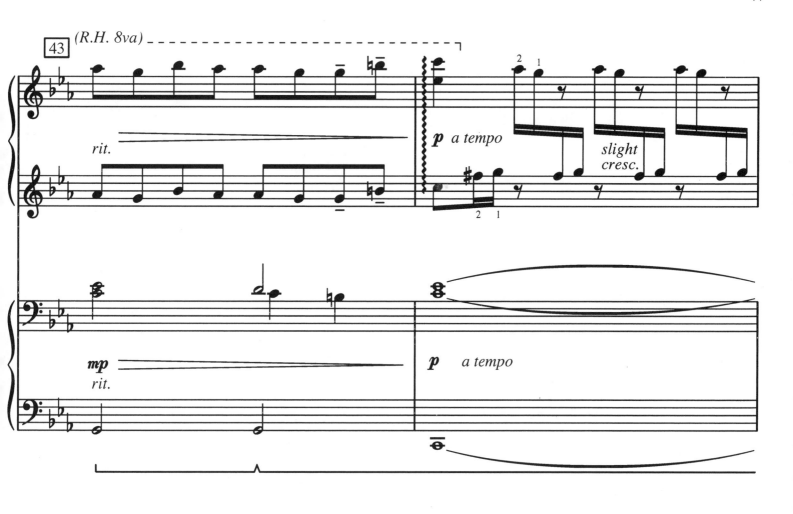

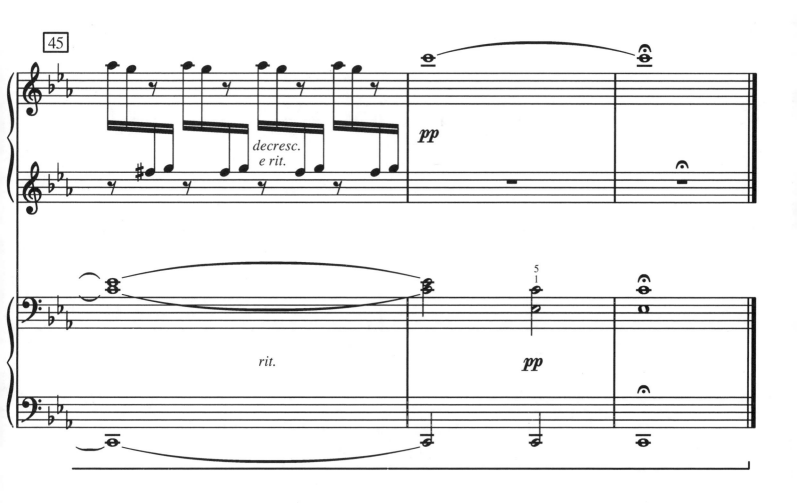

THE JOHN DUNBAR THEME
from DANCES WITH WOLVES

By JOHN BARRY

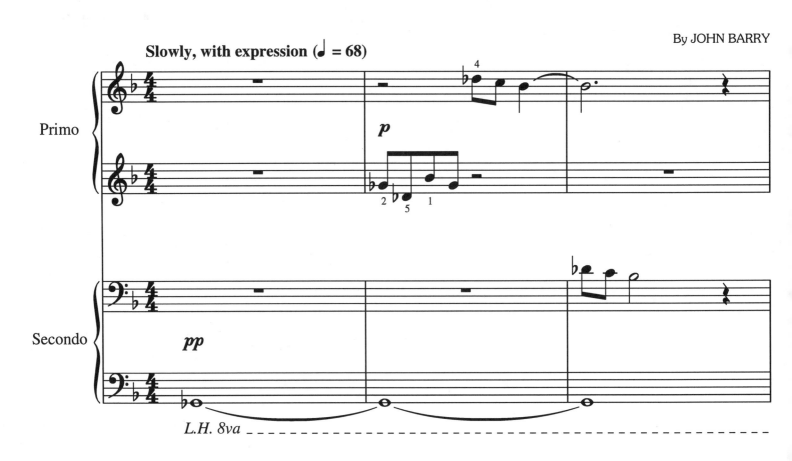

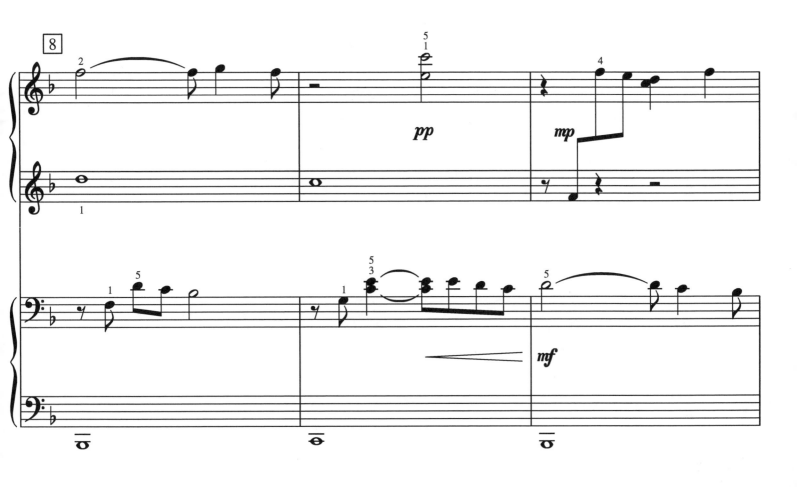

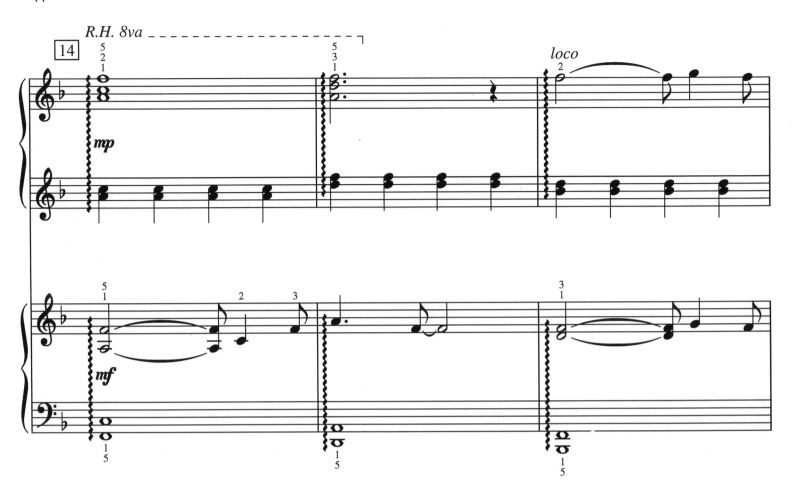

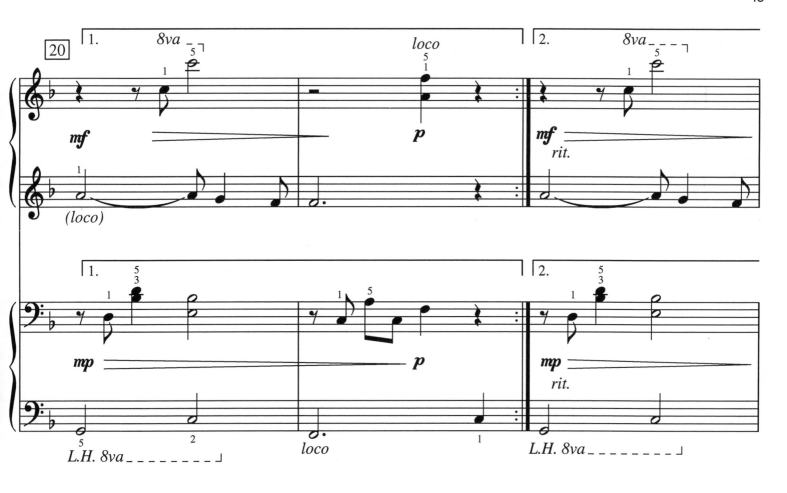

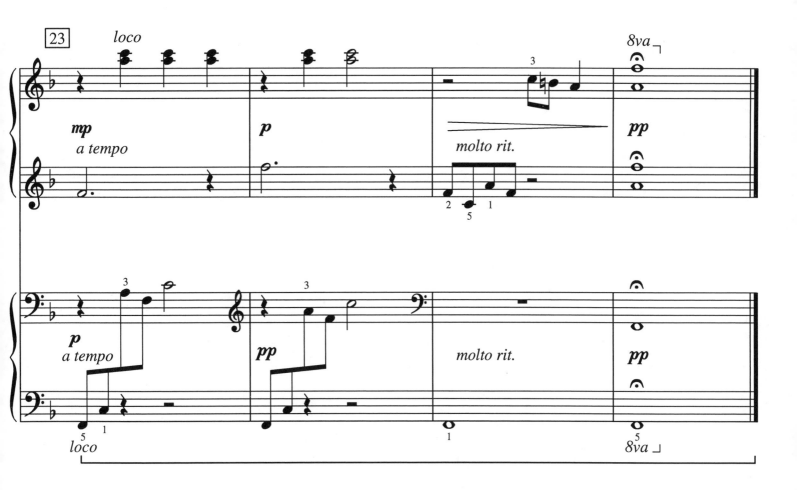

MOON RIVER
from the Paramount Picture BREAKFAST AT TIFFANY'S

Words by JOHNNY MERCER
Music by HENRY MANCINI

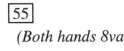

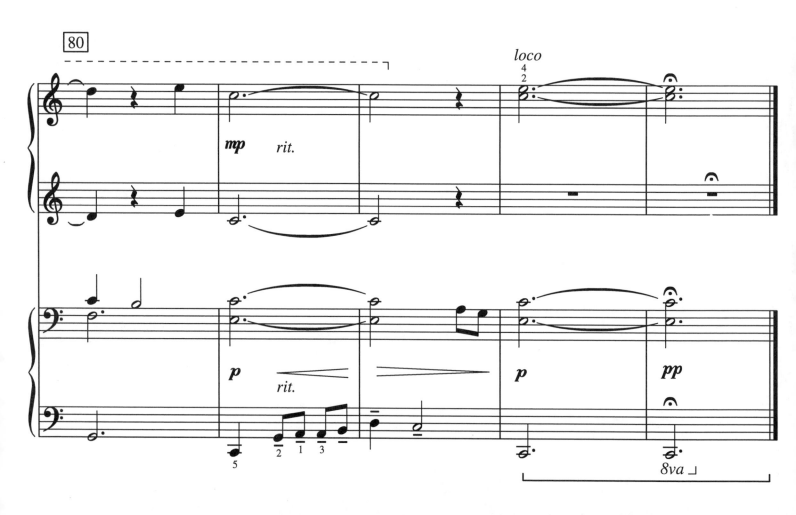

ROMEO AND JULIET
(Love Theme)
from the Paramount Picture ROMEO AND JULIET

By NINO ROTA

2nd time, R.H. 8va - - - - - - - - - - - - - - - -

THEME FROM "SCHINDLER'S LIST"

from the Universal Motion Picture SCHINDLER'S LIST

Composed by JOHN WILLIAMS

Slowly, with expression (♩ = 52)

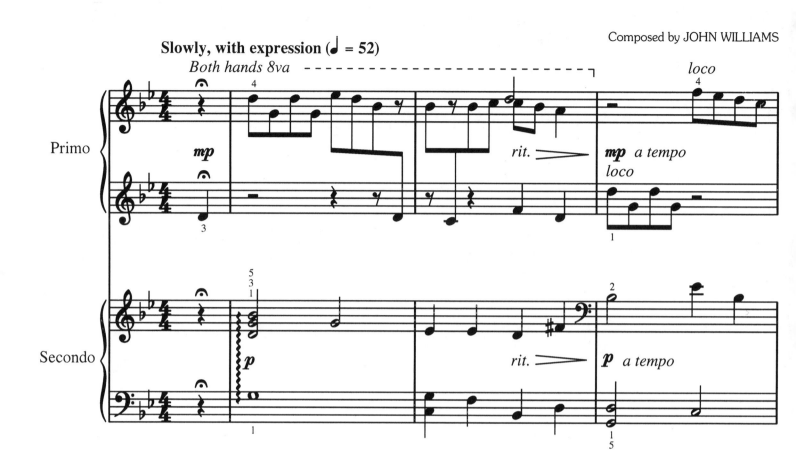

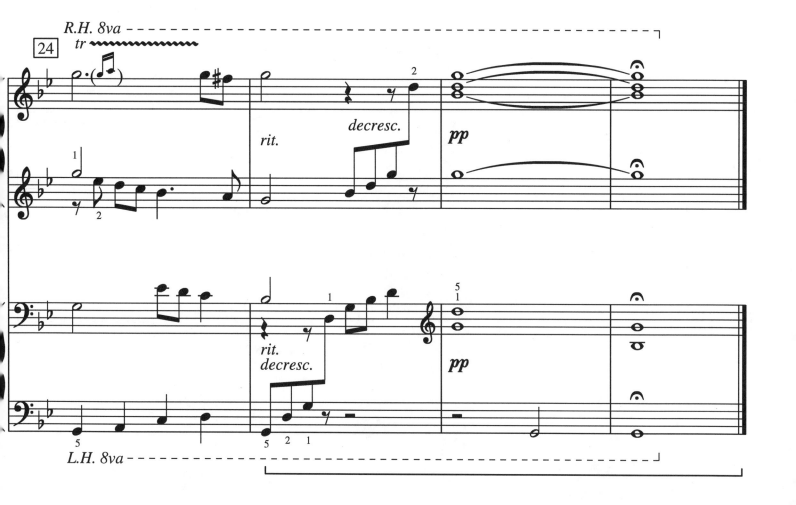

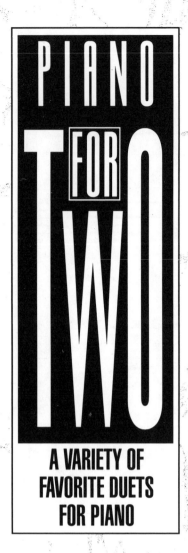

PIANO FOR TWO

A VARIETY OF FAVORITE DUETS FOR PIANO

ANDREW LLOYD WEBBER PIANO DUETS
8 of his best, including: All I Ask Of You • Don't Cry For Me Argentina • Memory • Superstar • and more.
00290332 ....$9.95

BROADWAY FAVORITES
8 of Broadway's best. Includes: All I Ask Of You • I Dreamed A Dream • I Got Plenty Of Nuttin' • Just In Time • Memory • On A Clear Day • People.
00290185 ....$6.95

CONTEMPORARY CHRISTIAN CLASSICS
12 songs, including: El Shaddai • How Majestic Is Your Name • People Need The Lord • We Are So Blessed.
00240980 ....$8.95

DISNEY TREASURES DUETS
8 Disney favorites, including: It's A Small World • Once Upon A Dream • Supercalifragilisticexpialidocious.
00240199 ....$6.95

DUET CLASSICS
A wonderful collection of 8 classics. Includes: Funeral March Of A Marionette • Humoresque • Liebestraum • Minuet In G (Beethoven) • and more.
00290172 ....$6.95

GEORGE GERSHWIN PIANO DUETS
10 classic Gershwin tunes, including: Summertime • A Foggy Day • It Ain't Necessarily So • They Can't Take That Away From Me • and more.
00312603 ....$6.95

COLE PORTER PIANO DUETS
6 of Porter's best. Includes: Rosalie • I Love Paris • Do I Love You? • From This Moment On • Allez-Vous-En, Go Away • In The Still Of The Night.
00312680 ....$5.95

ROCK N' ROLL PIANO DUETS
8 all-time rock 'n' roll favorites. Includes: All I Have To Do Is Dream • Blue Suede Shoes • Blueberry Hill • Don't Be Cruel • Only You (And You Alone) • Put Your Head On My Shoulder • Rock Around The Clock • Shake, Rattle And Roll.
00290171 ....$6.95

Prices subject to change without notice. Prices will vary outside the U.S.A. Not all products are available outside the U.S.A.

FOR MORE INFORMATION, SEE YOUR LOCAL MUSIC DEALER, OR WRITE TO:

HAL•LEONARD™ CORPORATION
7777 W. BLUEMOUND RD. P.O. BOX 13819 MILWAUKEE, WI 53213